AUDREY 100

A rare and intimate photo collection selected by Audrey Hepburn's family

AUDREY 100

A rare and intimate photo collection selected by Audrey Hepburn's family

by Ellen Fontana
Foreword by Sean Hepburn Ferrer

METRO BOOKS

NEW YORK

© 2010 by Sean Hepburn Ferrer and Luca Dotti

This 2011 edition published by Metro Books,
by arrangement with becker&mayer! LLC

Design: Joanna Price
Editorial: Kristin Mehus-Roe
Image Research: Shayna Ian
Production Coordination: Diane Ross

Cover image credits:
Front cover: Photo courtesy of mptvimages.com
Back cover: Photo by Antony Beauchamp / Audrey Hepburn Estate Collection
© Sean Ferrer and Luca Dotti
Please see image credits on page 190 for copyright information

Metro Books
122 Fifth Avenue
New York, NY 10011

ISBN: 978-1-4351-2725-8

Library of Congress Cataloging-in-Publication Data Available

Printed and bound in China

3   5   7   9   10   8   6   4   2

We dedicate this collection to everyone who helped make Audrey Hepburn the icon that she is — to her new and old fans, the photographers, the filmmakers, the humanitarians who helped and inspired her, her friends and family, and last but not least, the children of the world who she so desired to save.

Foreword

HOW DOES ONE CHOOSE THE 100 BEST PHOTOGRAPHS of one of the most photographed women of our time? I often wondered, when the time came to take pictures at Christmas, why my mother always preferred to be the one taking the shot and rushed through those including her. Now—after years of caring for her image and likeness and poring over literally thousands of images of her—I know. I have come to understand what a photograph meant to her.

To my mother, a photo was not what it may be to one of us—a memento, a way to record a moment in time that we will want to relive later on when everyone has scattered. To her it was hard work. A photo was a conjunction of factors that would immortalize perfection: the best photographers, designers, lighting, makeup, and hair; the right amount of sleep, luck, magic—and her, looking as though all of it was thoroughly enjoyable and effortless. It represented as much effort and energy as went into a whole day of shooting a film. In some cases, the photo would be used for the artwork of a film's poster or become its iconic link—it would carry all of the weight of months or even years of a film's creation, preparation, production, post-production, and marketing—not to speak of the millions invested in its creation and distribution.

And she took it just that seriously. As if, she used to say, "her life depended on it"—and the lives of all of those who had poured large chunks of their lives into its birth. My mother's photographs were a far cry from our "family snaps."

When my mother put her career on hold to raise us, her sons, it was also to be a pleasant vacation from the taking of these pictures. She resented the paparazzi in Rome and often told us that she felt bad that somehow their need—their desire—to capture her might somehow encroach on our private lives. This was indeed a highly sensitive perspective but she was probably also projecting her own anguish about it on to us. We simply didn't care at first, and then we thought of it as kind of fun.

How interesting that after all these years this huge body of photographic work is still one of the pillars of her presence—her legacy—along with her films. It is true that nothing can replace a photograph; it really does speak more than a thousand words. Without them, she wouldn't—couldn't—continue to be regarded as the fashion icon that she still is. And the work of Hubert de Givenchy, Edith Head, Valentino, Ralph Lauren, and most importantly Cecil Beaton, Hans Gerber, Pierluigi Praturlon, Philippe Halsman, Emil Schulthess, Sam Shaw, Norman Parkinson, Leo Fuchs, Willy Rizzo, David Seymour, Yousuf Karsh, Douglas Kirkland, Inge Morath, Marcel Imsand, Ove Wallin, Antony Beauchamp, Howell Conant, Bob Willoughby, Sanford Roth, Betty Press, Marc Shaw, John Engstead, Inge Morath, and John Isaac would be lost forever. How interesting that something that caused her such anguish and stress could have a long-lasting repercussion of such legendary proportions.

So here we were with the impossible task of selecting these images. How does one choose the best, and by what standard? And how could we leave images out that still told a story but maybe were not perfect from a technical standpoint, either because of the circumstances, the light, the lack of makeup, the circles under the eyes, the less flattering side? Perhaps these photos were even more valuable than the usual "expected" perfection.

I thought of those images that my father took, that barely hid the exhaustion of years of grueling personal and professional schedules or, sometimes, even her melancholy. But it was my brother Luca, a wonderful graphic artist, who made that quarter-of-an-inch adjustment to our route that sent us miles off course from our original destination—to a much happier one!

Luca took the pressure off the beauty and perfection aspect of the selection and refocused it on the story. Each image would tell a story and together they would tell yet another. Their beauty would lie in the emotions that they conveyed rather than in their technical perfection. And why not? Why should photos be treated any other way than a good book, a film, or a work of art?

Sometimes little independent films touch our hearts more so than those blockbusters brimming with stars, just as a man picks up a pen and writes his first book—his only book—and captures the imagination of our global consciousness. One man's mess is another man's masterpiece.

I am starting to repeat myself; this is what I said when I wrote the preface to *The Audrey Hepburn Treasures*. But it is, yet again, a matter of what will emerge between the lines—and in the case of that book what emerged between the documents. In this instance, what will emerge between the images?

I remember, when I was a boy, one of my teachers explained why literature would never be replaced by films or television. He believed that what made books the ultimate and irreplaceable form of communication and entertainment was the fact that we the readers created the visuals, the images—the film—in our own minds, just the way we wanted it. In this case, you will write the story, putting together what you already know about Audrey Hepburn with the emotions, the feelings, and the smiles.

So we present to you 100 graphic words, 100 emotions, 100 feelings, 100 little pieces of time. Uncluttered by too many explanations—clear and digestible—ready for you to assimilate directly into your soul. Once you have felt your way through it—a few times—slowly a new image will begin to emerge: a work of art dedicated to her life, her joys, her sorrows, her mischievousness, her laughter. But it will never be final. As you change, it will change with you—and stay with you. It is our hope that this book will embrace you and allow you to maintain a connection to this most lovely person—Audrey. *Audrey 100* is only a title—just words. With this collection we want to thank you—she wants to thank you—and say to you everything that just words cannot express.

—*Sean Hepburn Ferrer*

the photographs

The photographs in *Audrey 100* were chosen by the three men Audrey Hepburn was closest to in her lifetime: her sons, Sean and Luca, and her beloved partner, Rob Wolders. Sean, Luca, and Rob pored over thousands of photographs of Audrey before choosing the 100 images that are now before you. Each closely considered every photograph for its beauty, artistry, and ability to convey the person behind the movie star; the process triggered dialogue and debate. Sean asks in his foreword, "How does one choose the 100 best photographs of one of the most photographed women of our time?" With consideration and patience, as well as a great deal of resolve, it seems. Ultimately, not every photograph that matters could be included, and not every photograph was agreed upon by every participant. But every photo represents a moment in Audrey's life that her family was generous enough to share.

Audrey Hepburn Estate Collection, circa 1951

For dear Audrey Hepburn
with love
Joan & Bill Collins

'10·X·89

P.S × Thank you

Cecil Beaton, 1963

Cecil Beaton, 1963

Cecil Beaton, 1954

Cecil Beaton, 1954

To Audrey
with Best from
Cecil

Hans Gerber, circa 1954

Pierluigi Praturlon, 1959

Following pages (24–25): Philippe Halsman, 1955; Emil Schulthess, date unknown

Audrey Hepburn Estate Collection, 1963

Sam Shaw, 1956

Norman Parkinson, 1955

Mel Ferrer, date unknown

Leo Fuchs, 1958

Best wishes
Audrey
Hepburn

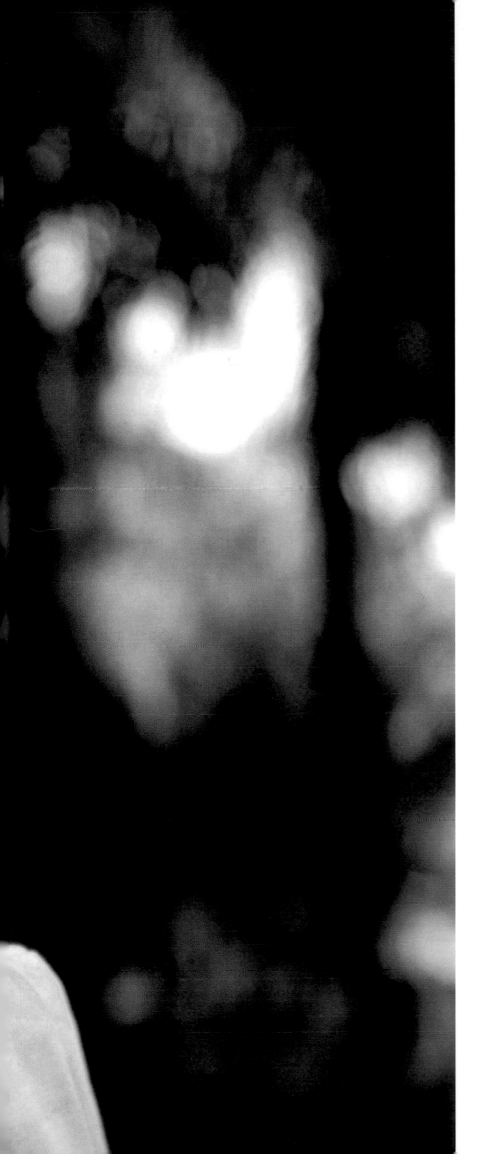

Leo Fuchs, 1958

Leo Fuchs, 1958

Cecil Beaton, 1963

Following pages (44–45): Audrey Hepburn Estate Collection, 1956; Willy Rizzo, 1956

David Seymour, 1954

48

Cecil Beaton, 1964

Beaton

Yousuf Karsh, 1956

Audrey Hepburn Estate Collection, 1956

Mark Shaw, 1953

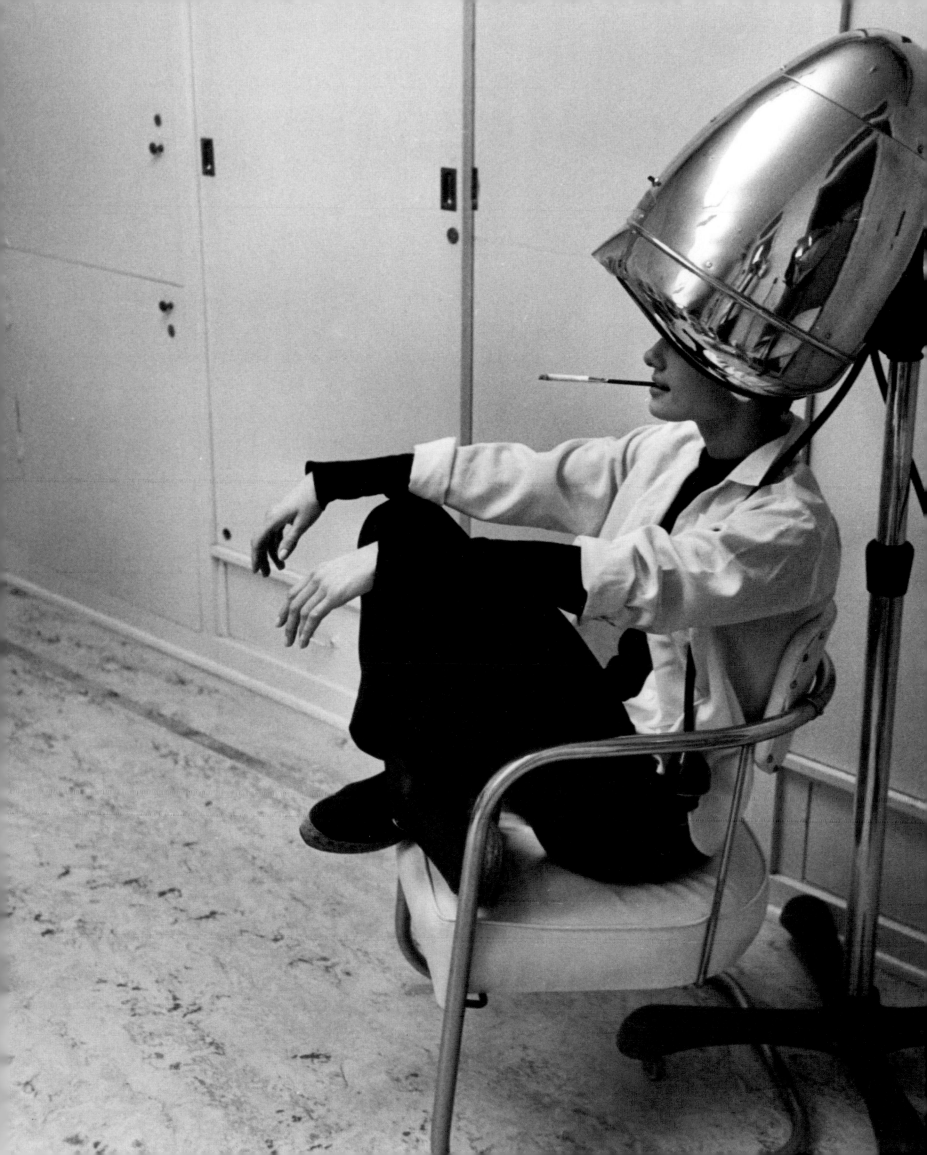

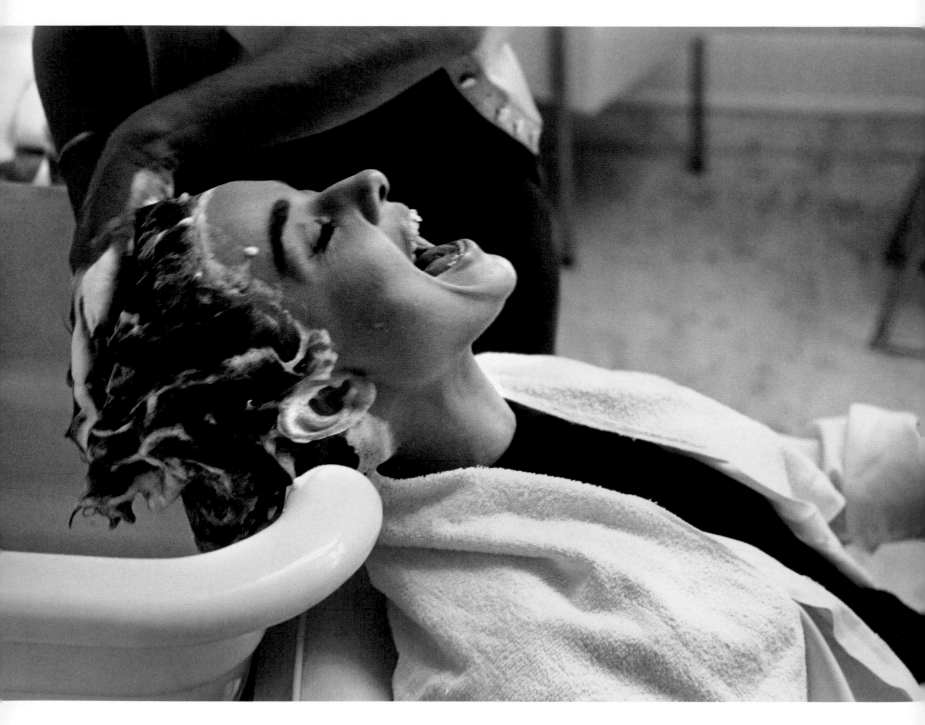

Mark Shaw, 1953

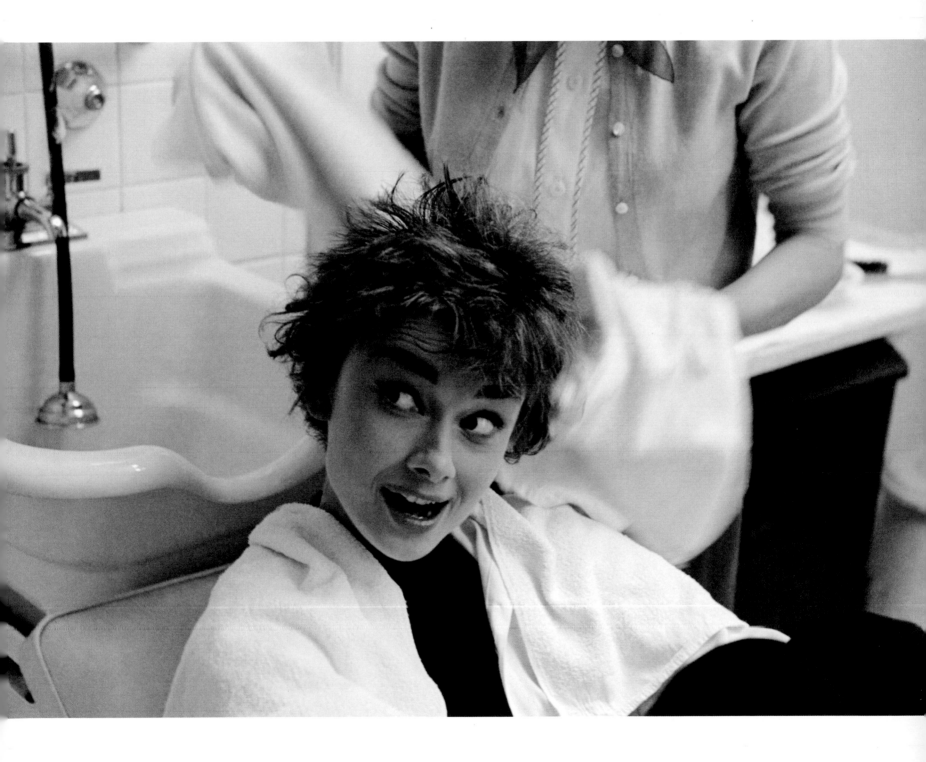

Mel Ferrer, 1954

Sam Shaw, 1956

Audrey Hepburn Estate Collection, 1954

Douglas Kirkland, 1965

Douglas Kirkland, 1965

Paramount Pictures, 1960

Photographer unknown, 1961

Following pages (74–75): Inge Morath, 1959

Opposite: Photographer unknown, 1961; Above: Photographer unknown, 1961

Audrey Hepburn Estate Collection, 1961

Philippe Halsman, 1955

Philippe Halsman, 1955

84

Pierluigi Praturlon, 1965

Mark Shaw, 1953

Norman Parkinson, 1955

Audrey Hepburn Estate Collection, circa 1963

Pierluigi Praturlon, 1965

Leo Fuchs, 1958

Audrey Hepburn Estate Collection, 1959

Marcel Imsand, 1969

Ove Wallin, date unknown

Antony Beauchamp, 1955

Above: Mel Ferrer, date unknown; Opposite: Audrey Hepburn Estate Collection, date unknown

Audrey Hepburn Estate Collection, 1955

Audrey Hepburn Estate Collection, 1955

Paramount Pictures, 1956

Howell Conant, 1958

Bob Willoughby, 1953

116

Mark Shaw, 1953

Mark Shaw, 1953

Photographer unknown, circa 1956

Mark Shaw, 1953

Photographer unknown, 1954

126

Bob Willoughby, circa 1958

Mel Ferrer, date unknown

Above: John Springer Collection, 1956; Opposite: Photographer unknown, 1956

Bob Willoughby, 1958

Photographer unknown, 1959

Opposite: Audrey Hepburn Estate Collection, 1953; Above: Bob Willoughby, 1953

Douglas Kirkland, 1965

Audrey Hepburn Estate Collection, circa 1970

Mark Shaw, 1954

Philippe Halsman, 1955

Mark Shaw, 1953

John Engstead, 1953

Bob Willoughby, 1958

Mel Ferrer, 1954

Douglas Kirkland, circa 1975

Sanford Roth, circa 1958

Betty Press, 1992

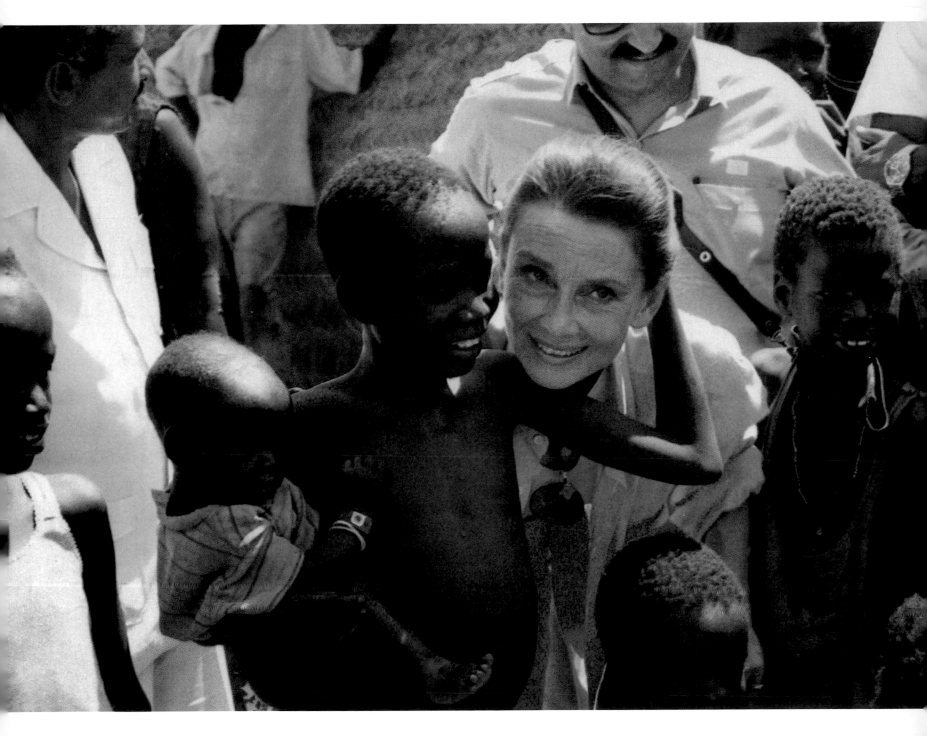

Robert Wolders, 1989

John Isaac, 1988

Robert Wolders, 1991

the captions

The 100 photographs in this collection convey more than 100 stories. Some suggest the complex emotions of a woman whose childhood was rooted in war and deprivation. Others contain memories that are cherished by her friends and family. Still others were selected because of their simple beauty. The following captions, combining the reflections of Rob, Sean, and Luca, as well as the photographers who photographed Audrey and the perceptions of her public, attempt to provide a context for the stories beyond those conveyed by the images.

10–11: Audrey Hepburn Estate Collection, circa 1951

In 1951, director Thorold Dickinson was still holding auditions for the part of Nora in *The Secret People* even as shooting on the film began. One reason that casting was so difficult was that most of the dancers auditioning for Nora's part were taller than co-stars Valentina Cortese and Serge Reggiani. Upon watching Audrey, Cortese (seated at the piano in this still from the movie) remarked, "I saw at the barre this beautiful little thing, like a little deer, with this long neck and those big eyes," and implored Dickinson to hire her. Ultimately Cortese made sure Audrey got the role by having Audrey remove her shoes for the screen test while she [Valentina] stood on tiptoes to equalize their height.

12–13: Cecil Beaton, 1963

When Beaton unveiled his sketchbook of costume designs for *My Fair Lady*, Audrey was delighted and exclaimed, "Oh, it's more than I thought it could possibly be. It's too much!" It is a testament to Audrey's natural grace and beauty that she looks equally at ease as both an impoverished flower girl and a high-society sophisticate. For his efforts on *My Fair Lady*, Beaton received two Academy Awards, for art direction and costume design.

14–15: Cecil Beaton, 1963

Here, Audrey models for Beaton in some of the creations actually designed for the extras in the movie's high-society scenes. These photographs, taken by Beaton, are a sampling of the over one thousand he took of Audrey during the production of *My Fair Lady*. Beaton conjured up four hundred spectacular black-and-white costumes for the Ascot and ballroom scenes, designs that were highly detailed and idiosyncratic. Each costume required the actors to pay special attention to the construction so that their stylized movements would seem lyrical and effortless.

17: Cecil Beaton, 1954

"Composed grace and nostalgia were Mum's traits," Luca remarks, qualities Beaton epitomizes in this quietly sensitive portrait of Audrey. Beaton understood what Audrey brought to his lens, aptly characterizing her as having "a waifish, poignant sympathy." Taken by Audrey's "long unvarnished nails," he chose to feature them in this photo. "She wears no powder," he said, "so that her white skin has a bright sheen." He called Audrey's unique presence "an almost Oriental sense of the exquisite."

18–19: Cecil Beaton, 1954

Beaton first met Audrey on July 23, 1953, at her flat on South Audley Street in London. Beaton was greeted warmly by Audrey's mother, Ella Van Heemstra, and, while Audrey finished dressing, he was graciously offered hors d'oeuvres and a martini. Upon their meeting, Beaton later recalled that, "without any of the preliminaries I felt that she cut through to a basic understanding that makes people friends. Nothing had to be explained: we liked one another. A chord had been struck and I knew that, next time we met, we would continue straight from here with no recapitulation of formalities. This was a unique occasion." These two autographed photos were given as a gift of friendship to Audrey from Cecil Beaton.

20–21: Hans Gerber, circa 1954

Taken on Lake Lucerne in Switzerland, Audrey holds the reins of the colorful speedboat like a rodeo pro. These photos are from a series taken for the August 1954 issue of *Schweizer Illustrierte Zeitung* (*Pictorial Parade*), accompanied by a feature article on Audrey. Lake Lucerne had significant meaning and memories for Audrey. It is here where her civil marriage ceremony to Mel took place and where the couple spent precious days sailing and relaxing with close friends and family.

23: Pierluigi Praturlon, 1959

Pierluigi captures Audrey in a moment of serene delight. As one of Italy's top film-set photographers, Pierluigi broke away from the accepted norm of posing stars, opting instead to reveal them more authentically. Thus, in many ways, Pierluigi became a master of what Luca refers to as "the surprise of being there." This Pierluigi moment captures Audrey on the terrace of her suite at the Hotel Hassler in Rome. The telegram she holds conveys the news that she's been voted Best Actress of 1959 for *The Nun's Story* by the New York Film Critics Circle as reported in *Film Daily*.

"This is where it all started," Sean says of the Hotel Hassler, "with Greg, Willy, and an ice cream cone . . . And Pierluigi—the ultimate paparazzo and a wonderful friend."

24: Philippe Halsman, 1955

Audrey's ballet training pays off as she jumps hedge high for photographer Philippe Halsman. In what he coined "jumpology," Halsman ended many of his celebrity photo sessions by asking his subjects to jump. "When you ask a person to jump," Halsman said, "his attention is mostly directed toward the act of jumping and the mask falls so that the real person appears. . . . They reveal whether they are rigid, fun, or mentally unstable." Here Audrey displays the sheer joy of being airborne. Taken over a six-year period, Halsman's collection of 178 jumpers, including Audrey, was published in 1959.

25: Emil Schulthess, date unknown

As a photographer, Emil Schulthess was naturally drawn to science and nature and, in 1957, began publishing photo essays on Africa, Antarctica, the Amazon, China, and the Soviet Union. Wherever he was, his aim was "to display various secrets of nature and to show the diversity of human life." Here he seems to capture Audrey mid-thought as she weaves together a delicate chain of clover. Luca calls this photo "the original recipe that started it all—because there wasn't one." Of Schulthess, Sean remarks, "Emil was a gentle man and the photographer of nature. . . . This photo was taken during the summer in Bürgenstock, Switzerland, where I was born."

27: Condé Nast Archive, 1963

Audrey pedals on the back lot with her Yorkie named Assam of Assam. The inseparable duo was captured here on Audrey's preferred mode of transportation—her bicycle—shuttling between sets. Assam was Audrey's second Yorkie, given to her in Paris by Mel after her beloved Famous was killed by a car in Los Angeles. "She was ga-ga over all the dogs that she had, and she always had one," Director Billy Wilder said.

28–29: Audrey Hepburn Estate Collection, 1963

Audrey and husband, Mel Ferrer, are juxtaposed in this photo cleverly shot as if they were perching atop the boxing ring ropes. With her raincoat slung over the far corner behind them, the couple takes time out to clown for the camera in New York City. There they starred opposite each other in *Mayerling*, a romantic tragedy that was part of the popular television series *Producers' Showcase*. "Just love this shot and its contradictions—the ring versus the fun," says Luca.

"I love to see them laughing," Sean says of his parents. "There was joy."

31: Sam Shaw, 1956

"Magically perfect innocence," is how Sean characterizes this photo of his mother taken by Sam Shaw. Here Audrey's simple glance seems to penetrate right through Shaw's lens. In her gloved hands, she holds Famous, her first Yorkie, who was seldom out of her sight. Especially well known for his portraits of women, Shaw photographed Audrey several times over a period of four years.

32–33: Norman Parkinson, 1955

Norman Parkinson was a fashion photographer with a career that lasted more than seventy years. He shot many of the world's famous and infamous notables du jour. "A photographer working without a magazine behind him is like a farmer without fields," Parkinson once said, which explains why so many *Vogue* covers in the 1950s were his. Here, Parkinson pairs Audrey with a donkey whose leash she's wrapped around her ankle. An avid animal lover, Audrey seems to have found a kindred spirit in her diminutive friend, who seems much more interested in looking at her than toward the camera.

34–35: Mel Ferrer, date unknown

Mel Ferrer captures his wife relaxed, smiling, and ready for the sun. "My Dad and his Rolleiflex . . . ," Sean says, pointing out that his Mum has "no makeup, no hair, no costume —truly 'homemade.' " A prolific actor, writer, director, and producer, Mel had a natural flair and affinity for the camera. He enjoyed taking candid shots of Audrey and all the family, many of which are among the most precious images in the Hepburn Estate Archive.

37: Leo Fuchs, 1958

"I love all the series by Leo Fuchs. I don't think Mum ever looked any better," Luca comments. Shot on location in the Belgian Congo during the filming of *The Nun's Story*, Audrey and Fuchs became good friends and often spent the evenings together listening to Beethoven. Fuchs's style of shooting celebrities rendered more natural-feeling portraits and thus conveyed "a quieter kind of myth-making," according to one article about him. This particular photo was chosen by Audrey and autographed to be mailed out to requesting fans. Sean recalls: "Boxes of it [the photo] were printed and my parents' assistant, Margaret Brown, bless her soul, diligently sent them out."

38–39: Leo Fuchs, 1958

Fuchs manages to capture Audrey looking unaffected by the 130-degree heat of the Belgian Congo. Unlike some of her co-stars who suffered heatstroke, Audrey credited her nun's habit with protecting her from the heat during filming. She did, however, succumb to a terrible case of kidney stones upon returning to Rome to finish the arduous 132-day shoot. Once fully recovered, Audrey finished the film and was nominated for a Best Actress Academy Award for her performance as Sister Luke.

41: Leo Fuchs, 1958

Looking perfectly at ease, Audrey strolls the street under the shady protection of an umbrella. "A tan can ruin the continuity of one's makeup," Sean notes, adding, "It's always easy to add it, but almost impossible to cover it up."

43: Cecil Beaton, 1963

With a natural flair for the dramatic, the great Cecil Beaton places Audrey in fierce shadow and light on the set of *My Fair Lady*. "It has been repeated," Sean notes, "that when the Queen Mother first saw my mother, she leaned over to Princess Anne and whispered, 'She's one of us.'" Beaton's semi-silhouetted rendering of Audrey adorned in regalia offers proof positive of the royal sentiment.

44: Audrey Hepburn Estate Collection, 1956

Audrey has a moment of levity during a dance rehearsal for *Funny Face*. Starring opposite Fred Astaire, Audrey was well aware that he was the most popular dancer of his day and, to millions of women, represented the male ideal—the epitome of the suave, sophisticated gentleman. On the morning of their first rehearsal, Audrey remembered she was "so shaken I threw up my breakfast . . . I was absolutely terrified, but Fred said, 'Honey, just follow me, I'll take care of everything.' And he did."

45: Willy Rizzo, 1956

Despite the fact that the war had robbed Audrey of her dreams of becoming a prima ballerina, she managed to maintain the discipline and body consciousness instilled in her from years of serious training. Audrey modestly claimed, "I had a very slender kind of technique." Be that as it may, she utilized that technique to the nth degree in *Funny Face* during her avant-garde dance solo, "Basal Metabolism," and in all the romantic dance sequences with co-star Fred Astaire. Photographer Willy Rizzo, who had a personal passion for dance, was on set and in rehearsals for *Funny Face*.

47: David Seymour, 1954

Audrey wears a wedding gown and veil in her role as Jo Stockton in *Funny Face*. The photo was taken by David Seymour, who, in 1947, helped found the first international cooperative photographic agency—Magnum. The dance scene in which Audrey wears this costume was shot outdoors after weeks of torrential rain. Audrey had nine pairs of white satin dancing shoes that were made in Paris that she had to continuously swap out as each became muddied beyond use. "Here I've been waiting twenty years to dance with Fred Astaire," Audrey quipped, "and what do I get? Mud in my eye!"

48–49: Cecil Beaton, 1964

In this Beaton photo of Audrey, he compels the viewer's eye to notice everything he wants it to. Beaton's use of the curved Moroccan teapot and the painted paisley directs the viewer's immediate attention to Audrey. Her delicately placed hand, purposely held up by the other, the fingertips that barely touch the corner of the tray, her fixed glance, and enigmatic mouth are all deliberate and precise and demonstrate Audrey's great trust in Beaton and his in her to deliver his artistic vision.

50: Cecil Beaton, 1955

In contrast to Beaton's own flamboyant personal sense of style and manner, his portraits often highlight a certain quiet sense of reserve and formality, such as in this signed portrait taken of Audrey in 1955.

51: Cecil Beaton, 1964

"Be daring, be different, be impractical, be anything that will assert integrity of purpose and imaginative vision against the play-it-safers, the creatures of the commonplace, the slaves of the ordinary."—Cecil Beaton

Here Beaton captures an "imaginative vision" of Audrey in Givenchy for the August 15, 1964, issue of *Vogue*. "Design + model + photographer," says Luca. "The result outdoes the sum of the parts."

53: Yousuf Karsh, 1956

Yousuf Karsh, one of the greatest portrait photographers of all time, remembered meeting and working with Audrey in 1956. "When I photographed her in Hollywood and commented on her quality of sophisticated vulnerability," Karsh said, "she told me of her harrowing experiences during the Second World War. Years later, in the Kremlin, Chairman Brezhnev agreed to sit for me only if I made him as beautiful as Audrey Hepburn."

Looking at Karsh's immaculate portrait of Audrey, Luca comments that, "Her Dutch origins show here so much. . . ." Sean adds, "She was the perfect combination of imperfections."

54–55: Audrey Hepburn Estate Collection, 1956

"I love this one," Luca says. "She looks like a teenager playing with clothes." Though both the story of the photo and photographer remain a mystery, Sean calls the mise-en-scène "organically true."

57: Mark Shaw, 1953

Audrey relaxes under the hair dryer during the filming of *Sabrina*, part of her daily transformation captured by photographer Mark Shaw. Gnawing on an elegant black cigarette holder, no one could have predicted that six years later this "prop" would help define Audrey's signature look as Holly Golightly.

"My mother taught me to stand straight, sit erect, and to smoke only six cigarettes a day," Audrey stated. And it was her mother who sent her the cigarette holder purchased at the Dunhill Shop in London, tobacconist to George VI and Sir Winston Churchill.

58–59: Mark Shaw, 1953

"Mark Shaw caught Audrey in one of her deliciously clownish outbursts—a side of her very familiar to family and friends but, regrettably, not sufficiently exploited in her movie roles," says Rob Wolders.

Luca also delights in seeing his mother mug for the camera "I still remember when many years ago I first saw this series of photos and thought, 'Wow, Mum was once a child!'"

60–61: Mel Ferrer, 1954

Audrey's expressions run the gamut, from cut-up to contemplative, in this series of photos taken by husband Mel while sailing on Lake Lucerne in Switzerland. Mel, in particular, loved being on the lake and frequented it every available weekend. Seated in profile near Audrey is family friend Fritz Frye.

"We lived in Villa Bethania on the Bürgenstock, which Fritz Frye rented to us," explains Sean, who last visited Villa Bethania in 1993.

"I would like people to relate more to the Audrey that comes out of these shots," Luca says.

62–63: Sam Shaw, 1956

These photos were taken by Sam Shaw during what Sean calls "the infamous *Love in the Afternoon* picnic scene, which took ten days to shoot." Billy Wilder directed Audrey and co-star Gary Cooper in this romantic escapade in which Audrey, playing Ariane, whines, "I'm too thin and my ears stick out and my teeth are crooked and my neck is much too long." These were complaints Audrey often made about herself in real life.

"Maybe so," says Cooper in the role of Frank Flannagan, "but I love the way it all hangs together."

65: Audrey Hepburn Estate Collection, 1954

Audrey beams at the Grand Hotel in Rome on September 29, 1954, on the occasion of her first public appearance as Mrs. Mel Ferrer. Audrey and Mel had wed five days earlier in Switzerland in two separate ceremonies, one civil and one religious, and began a brief honeymoon there. Upon arriving in Rome, the couple were followed by throngs of photographers. Not revealed in this version of the photo are the paparazzi surrounding the couple, as well as a few reporters squeezed in on the couch on both sides of them. The paparazzi were a force that Audrey had to deal with her entire career but ultimately learned to use effectively when it came to speaking out on behalf of her humanitarian work with UNICEF.

66–67: Douglas Kirkland, 1965

Photographer Douglas Kirkland got his first job working in a photo studio at the age of thirteen and never looked back. Eventually he found employment as a photographer's assistant to Irving Penn and went on to work as a staff photographer for both *Look* and *Life* magazines. This photo of Audrey is part of a series that was shot while she was working in Paris on *How to Steal a Million*. Kirkland, known for his ability to evoke the inner spirit of his subjects, has his own way of coaxing the essence of his subjects up to the surface of the photo. "If you want a beautiful woman to smile and look seductive, look into her eyes—project the feeling—and whisper," advises Kirkland. It's apparent here that Kirkland managed to "whisper" at Audrey's every angle.

69: Douglas Kirkland, 1965

Kirkland became a prolific Hollywood celebrity photographer and has been special photographer on 140 feature films. In this particular photo, Kirkland connects with what Rob Wolders calls Audrey's "impish" side.

"Audrey was delightful," Kirkland said, "and the easiest 'star' to photograph." Besides their warm and congenial working relationship, Kirkland also fondly remembers this session with Audrey because it was during the filming of *How to Steal a Million* that he was introduced to Françoise, his wife and partner of forty-three years.

70–71: Paramount Pictures, 1960

"When the cameraman has to absent himself, he usually asks someone to sit on the rig in his place," explains Sean. "Otherwise, because of the counterweight mechanism, the Chapman crane's boom would go flying straight up, sending the camera into orbit." Here, it is Audrey who sits on the rig in the stead of cinematographer Franz Planer, between takes on *Breakfast at Tiffany's*.

Audrey loved working with Franz and they made five films together—*Breakfast at Tiffany's*, *The Unforgiven*, *Roman Holiday*, *The Nun's Story*, and *The Children's Hour*, the last three of which earned him Oscar nominations.

73: Photographer unknown, 1961

"Somehow *Breakfast at Tiffany's* always makes me think that she never had the time to be spoiled in her real life," Luca remarks. "Everybody should be a little."

Audrey was nothing like her fictional counterpart, Holly Golightly. Raised with a Victorian upbringing, her mother taught Audrey to always think of others first and not to draw attention to herself. Thus, Audrey worried about playing Holly and confessed to her agent, Kurt Frings, that "Holly is so contrary to me. She frightens me. This part called for an extroverted character. I am an introvert." But as any seasoned agent knows, when an actor plays outside her comfort zone, the results often yield a spectacular performance. Audrey later remarked in an interview in 1964 that "playing the extroverted girl in *Breakfast at Tiffany's* was the hardest thing I ever did."

74–75: Inge Morath, 1959

Audrey's ballet training pays off again, as she rests with her beloved Yorkie, Assam, during the filming of *The Unforgiven*. "On a film set the lunch break is usually one hour," Sean explains. "Mum always took a quick lunch and then lay down for 45 minutes or so. If you've had to get up at 4:00 a.m., drive to the set to be in hair and makeup by 5:30, sit still for 60–90 minutes, be ready for a walk-through and rehearsal at 7:00 a.m., after which you have to get into wardrobe and get your first take in by 7:30 a.m.—it's understandable."

76: Photographer unknown, 1961

Ask anyone, anywhere around the world, what they remember best about Holly Golightly in *Breakfast at Tiffany's* and they will almost always say her clothes. Over the years Holly's iconic look for the film, designed by Hubert de Givenchy, became inseparable from the star herself. The classic tailored "Audrey Look" continues to be emulated, replete with the incomparable "little black dress." In 2006, Givenchy donated his personal version of Holly's gown to raise funds at auction for a charity located in India. The dress sold for over $923,000.

77: Photographer unknown, 1961

"Every actor has their sacred film," Sean says, pointing out that *Breakfast at Tiffany's* will forever be it for Audrey.

79: Audrey Hepburn Estate Collection, 1961

Although she must have been used to it by the time she spotted this store mannequin dressed to emulate her, the look on Audrey's face indicates it was still a peculiar experience. Proof lies on the floor of the store display where an actual head shot of Audrey is placed, which may have been used to inspire the window dresser.

80–83: Philippe Halsman, 1955

Audrey poses for Philippe Halsman on the grounds of the lovely farm called La Vigna, just outside of Rome, where he shot Audrey for the cover of the July 28, 1955, issue of *Life* magazine. Halsman had what Rob Wolders refers to as "a lifelong fascination with Audrey."

Halsman's "highly developed photographic insight allowed him to capture not only the nuances of his subject's face and being but even more what it was that each subject tried to conceal," says Rob.

84–85: Pierluigi Praturlon, 1965

On set at Studios de Boulogne in Paris, during the making of *How to Steal a Million*, Audrey sits in someone else's chair opposite director William Wyler. Wyler also directed Audrey in her American film debut, *Roman Holiday,* and in *The Children's Hour*. Like so many of Audrey's working associates, Willy became a dear lifelong friend whose guiding hand at the very beginning of Audrey's acting career and quest for perfection throughout were enormously valued and appreciated.

"He made her smile and he made her cry and she trusted him like family and loved him like an uncle," Sean says of Wyler.

87: Mark Shaw, 1953

Here with co-star William Holden on the set of *Sabrina*, Mark Shaw catches Audrey stifling a smile. "It leaves you guessing about what made her laugh," Luca says.

Although Audrey initially eschewed Shaw's lens, he eventually shot over sixty rolls of film of Audrey during the film's production. Shaw developed the day's work every evening and pored over the photos, intent on revealing the magic of Audrey's massive appeal.

Shaw's photo essay entitled "The Girl Behind the Glamour: Audrey Hepburn, Many-sided Charmer," appeared in a 1955 special publication of *Life* magazine called *How* Life *Gets the Story — Behind the Scenes in Photo-Journalism*.

89: Norman Parkinson, 1955

Taken at La Vigna, the charming farmhouse near Rome that Audrey and Mel rented during the location filming of *War and Peace*, Parkinson places Audrey in front of one of the farm's enormously prolific bougainvillea vines. Dressed in pale petal pink, Audrey's dress subtly echoes the natural color scheme surrounding her, offset by the simplest white gloves and pearls.

An altogether appealing juxtaposition by Parkinson, "who was known for changing the paradigm in fashion and lifestyle photography," says Rob.

91: Audrey Hepburn Estate Collection, circa 1963

"The face that launched a thousand cameras," Sean says of this photo. Taken during the production of *Charade*, Audrey was once again adorned in Givenchy's couture wardrobe.

The film reunited Audrey with director Stanley Donen, who also brought Cary Grant and James Coburn to co-star. The comedy caper movie is set in Paris and was written specifically for Audrey and Cary by Peter Stone. Audrey and Cary got along famously. "He had me down flat the minute he met me," she said of her co-star.

As for Cary, he once quipped, "All I want for Christmas is another movie with Audrey Hepburn." The film was nominated for a Best Music Oscar and Audrey won a Best Actress BAFTA for her work.

93: Pierluigi Praturlon, 1965

"I have often thought to myself, 'How do all of today's designers get up in the morning—with what courage?' Sort of like, 'Why write more classical music once Bach was done?!' Thank God for the French and their fear of *bowringh* and the Italians and their need for lunch!" quips Sean of this incomparable Pierluigi photo.

Wearing a white hat by Givenchy and trademark sixties sunglasses, Audrey easily carries another pared-down classic look to iconic stature.

95: Leo Fuchs, 1958

Taken in the Belgian Congo on location for *The Nun's Story*, Leo Fuchs snaps Audrey enjoying a light moment with an unseen table guest. Audrey also seeks to immortalize the moment herself, reaching for her own camera hanging around her neck.

"She would go back one day—with a different song in her heart," Sean said of Audrey and Africa, referring to the last five years of her life when Audrey undertook what she considered the privilege of becoming a UNICEF International Goodwill Ambassador. From 1988–1993, her UNICEF work took her around the world, including to war-torn Ethiopia, the Sudan, and, finally, to Somalia.

96–97: Audrey Hepburn Estate Collection, 1959

"Try this one on for size," suggests Sean. "Break your back in Mexico, far way from any hospital, then look this sweet and lovely while lying in the ambulance on your way to a plane which will fly you to the hospital in the U.S. where they will let you know If you'll ever walk again, all the while knowing that, at best, this has halted production of 'the film' for at least four to six weeks, or maybe forever. . . ." These were the circumstances after Audrey was thrown from her horse, Diablo, while filming *The Unforgiven*.

Typical of Audrey, she pleaded with husband Mel, "Don't get angry at the horse! It wasn't the horse's fault!" Luca recalls Audrey "joking about 'taking a break'" after her fall. He adds, that he, himself, was never allowed to ride a horse.

99: Marcel Imsand, 1969

Here Audrey smiles at the camera on the occasion of the "second try at the 'happiest day' of one's life," Sean jokes.

On January 18, 1969, Audrey and Andrea Dotti, a prominent Roman psychiatrist, wed in Morges, Vaud, Switzerland. Luca Dotti was born a little over a year later, nearly ten years after brother Sean.

Audrey's beatific glow outshone even the pink wool ensemble, made with love and best wishes by dear friend Hubert de Givenchy.

100–101: Ove Wallin, date unknown

This masterful photo might initially seem to be a double exposure but is actually a collage of images reflected on the window glass in the foreground, as well as seen through the window in the background of the car in which Audrey sits. Most likely this photo was taken as Audrey was about to ride to, or from, the set of *Breakfast at Tiffany's*. She is poised and ultra-focused, holding on with her gloved hand, ready for whatever lies ahead of her.

103: Antony Beauchamp, 1955

Audrey first met society photographer Antony Beauchamp in 1949, when she was working in a cabaret show in London called *Sauce Tartare*. Beauchamp, son-in-law of Winston Churchill, had seen Audrey perform and was immediately struck by her. "I couldn't quite fathom that she was real," he said, and offered to photograph her for a series he was doing on new faces. When asked, Audrey said she would be unable to because she could not afford to pay him for the sitting. Charmed, he insisted on the session regardless, for which Audrey later repaid him with an assignment as film-set photographer on *Roman Holiday*.

104: Mel Ferrer, date unknown

Audrey stands rooted in thought amid the tall bamboo stalks. "My father really did have the knack for catching the moment. It really goes to show that she couldn't take a bad pic!" says Sean.

105: Audrey Hepburn Estate Collection, date unknown

Sean believes this photo may have been taken in Spain. The beautiful balance of red and white and the detail of her hair ribbon make for a perfect candid shot. Perhaps the only thing out of place in the photo is the cigarette Audrey holds in her right hand.

"I have sins," Audrey said demurely about her smoking, which was still an accepted social custom at the time, on and off the set, when few realized the potential health risks.

106–107: Audrey Hepburn Estate Collection, 1955

"How can a hair and makeup test be that interesting!?" asks Sean, adding, "The camera did truly love her."

Here the test is for King Vidor's production of Tolstoy's *War and Peace*. The film's first draft script might be considered an epic in and of itself, coming in at a hefty 506 pages. In the stellar cast, which included both Audrey and Mel, was actor Jeremy Brett, who played Audrey's brother. Nearly eight years later, Brett would be cast again opposite Audrey, this time as her love interest in *My Fair Lady*. For *My Fair Lady*, Audrey received the highest salary ever paid to an actress to date. Quite humbled and embarrassed by the achievement, Audrey asked her agent to please not repeat the information.

108–109: Audrey Hepburn Estate Collection, 1955

Another set of hair tests for *War and Peace*. Tolstoy's epic story had been adapted for the screen multiple times but had never made it into production. In 1955, however, three different productions of the film were all gearing up and they all wanted Audrey to play Natasha. It was director King Vidor and Italian producing partners Dino De Laurentiis and Carlo Ponti who finally sealed the deal for Audrey and Mel.

Looking at these photos, Sean notes, "No makeup—she looks tired. Just imagine her schedule between *Roman Holiday* and *War and Peace*! Add press junkets, prep of eight to ten weeks per film, fashion shoots, appearances, and openings—personal life? Forget it!"

111: Paramount Pictures, 1956

"I think this Paramount publicity still highlights her grace and gentle nature," says Rob. Taken during the production of *Funny Face*, the photo shows Audrey dressed in her Givenchy Paris wardrobe, looking her iconic best.

For *Sabrina*, Edith Head was given the Costume Design credit leaving Givenchy unrecognized for his transformational Sabrina wardrobe. In *Funny Face*, Givenchy's austere credit read: Wardrobe: Miss Hepburn, Paris. *Funny Face* afforded a few surprising cameos, including high-fashion model Suzy Parker, whose life was the basis for Audrey's reluctant character; Audrey's mother, Ella; and Audrey's Yorkie, Famous.

113: Howell Conant, 1958

"When they said she might look elegant even if all she wore was a paper bag or a potato sack, they forgot a set of curtains!" says Sean, referring to the party scene in *Breakfast at Tiffany's*.

Here, in an impeccable Howell Conant photo, Audrey models a spectacular Givenchy gown. Hubert de Givenchy was a lifelong friend and confidant who said, "It was her inner beauty that made my clothes look so good."

When Audrey moved to her pastoral home in Switzerland, Givenchy sent her sixty Iceberg rose trees, renowned for their beauty and elegance. How appropriate. "Mum's grace always made her look like a 'debutante,'" Luca remarks.

115: Bob Willoughby, 1953

It was Bud Fraker, head portrait photographer at Paramount Pictures, who first introduced photographer Bob Willoughby to Audrey. Willoughby was sent to the studio by his agent to shoot a young upcoming starlet and thought it would be just another ordinary studio assignment. It turned out to be anything but ordinary. "She took my hand," Bob said, "and dazzled me with a smile that God designed to melt mortal men's hearts."

This photo was taken by Willoughby as Audrey got into the car taking her back to the Chapman Park Hotel on Wilshire Boulevard. As Sean so aptly points out, "Bob could catch it all, better than anyone."

116–117: Mark Shaw, 1953

Mark Shaw had unprecedented access to Audrey for two weeks during the making of *Sabrina*. Shaw captured many private moments when it seemed Audrey was genuinely unaware that he was there. Here, with pencil in hand, is one of those moments.

"Mum thought she was there by mistake," Luca says, "and woke up before 5:00 a.m. to work on her script."

Sean surmises that Audrey was probably "underlining the 'points' she had to make—creating the 'spine' of the scene. The trouble was," Sean says, "that she was done by take two—everyone else was just getting started!"

Shaw lovingly referred to Audrey as "The Monster," because of what he called her "rigid devotion" to her work.

119: Mark Shaw, 1953

Coasting toward the camera on the Paramount lot, Audrey takes a bike ride during a break in the filming of *Sabrina*. Shaw took a series of Audrey on her bike on different days in different outfits. "Most people think of Audrey Hepburn as regal," her former co-star Gregory Peck said. "I like to think of her as spunky."

121: Photographer unknown, circa 1956

Audrey didn't hesitate when it came to speaking about what she considered her short-comings—her flared nostrils, crooked teeth, and, particularly, her large feet. "She was always shy about her feet—too big," Sean says, "showing the ballet training."

Thus, when she did cover them, she was very particular about whom she wore—most notably Italian designer Salvatore Ferragamo and French designer René Mancini.

Here, in a rare moment, Audrey is captured ballet feet and all. "Audrey's seeming un-awareness of her natural beauty was so beguiling and disarming she could easily lead you to believe that she was just the girl next door," Rob says. Sitting atop the backyard picnic table, she seems to be just that.

Luca muses that this photo is "so airy it feels like she could sit on a leaf."

123: Mark Shaw, 1953

Audrey is captured between takes of the party scene where Sabrina gazes longingly at the festivities inside the mansion from her perch outside in a tree.

Filmed entirely on location in Glen Cove, Long Island, the movie was shot over nine weeks. Billy Wilder, who directed the film, recalled, "The very first day she came on the set prepared. She knew her lines. I did not have to squeeze it out of her. She was so gracious and graceful that everybody fell in love with her after five minutes."

125: Photographer unknown, 1954

This publicity still was taken at Paramount Pictures during the filming of *Sabrina*. In it, Audrey embodies the transformed Sabrina, no longer a chauffeur's daughter but a woman of the world.

Dressed for the occasion of a lavish Larabee party, Audrey attends unrecognized as the employee's daughter, wearing a spectacular black-and-white embroidered Givenchy ball gown and absolutely dazzles the Larabee guests, not to mention both Larabee brothers.

126–127: Bob Willoughby, circa 1958

This photo of Audrey and her dog Famous is part of a wonderful series shot by Willoughby in their home around 1958. Mel called Famous "a renowned scene-stealer."

The Ferrers chose one of Willoughby's photos to use as their 1958 Christmas card. That photo featured Audrey, Mel, Famous, and Ip, the fawn that Audrey brought home to bond with during the filming of *Green Mansions*. In March 2006, this photo appeared on the cover of *Architectural Digest* with the title banner, "Audrey Hepburn Remembered by Mel Ferrer."

128–129: Mel Ferrer, date unknown

This candid photo of Audrey was taken by Mel, sometime in the mid-1950s.

130: John Springer Collection, 1956

This photo from *Funny Face* shows Audrey's sophisticated demeanor both in style and attitude. Commanding the background is an enormous classic train that releases atmospheric steam behind Audrey, dressed spotlessly in classic Givenchy. Aside from her straw case, Audrey also holds Famous, her dog, who was a willing prop for the scene.

131: Photographer unknown, 1956

"I depend on Givenchy in the same way that American women depend on their psychiatrists," Audrey said. "His are the only clothes in which I am myself."

Thus, Givenchy would continue to design Audrey's movie wardrobes and his services were written into Audrey's contracts. "Audrey was the first actress to play a fashion model on screen who really could have been one off screen," *Funny Face* screenwriter Leonard Gershe noted. "The audience bought that she could be this creature."

132: Bob Willoughby, 1958

Audrey holds Ip, also known as Ippy and Pip, the fawn used during the filming of *Green Mansions*. Ip became an integrated member of the Ferrer family, actually living at the Ferrer home with Mel, Audrey, and Famous and sleeping in the family's bathtub. As for the fawn's acting abilities, Mel is quoted as having said, "I still cannot understand why Ippy did not deserve a nomination. He performed brilliantly."

Luca recalls, "Her love for the fawn finally broke her heart. She never stopped telling us how much sorrow she felt when they had to part. It also became one of her greatest legacies left to us: Nature is not a game to play with."

133: Bob Willoughby, 1958

The bond is evident between actress and co-star. Ip followed Audrey everywhere, accompanying her to the supermarket in Beverly Hills and to her beauty shop appointments. Audrey bottle fed Ip warm goat's milk every two hours and he ate with the family in the evening in the dining room.

"It was a sad day at the completion of shooting," Mel said, "when I had to drive him [Ip] out to an animal farm in the San Fernando Valley." One can only imagine.

134–135: Photographer unknown, 1959

"Add reading glasses and thirty-one years—the expression is the same—and we're at home in 1990," says Sean.

In one of Luca's favorite photos of his mother, Audrey sits on set of *The Unforgiven*, serenely slipping black cashmere wool between her delicate knitting needles. This photo was taken upon her return to the set after suffering a broken back during the production. Audrey used knitting to relax between scenes and favored making sweaters, shawls, and even socks for husband Mel. A reference to Audrey's knitting can be found in *Wait Until Dark* when Richard Crenna's character, Mike, picks up an unfinished sweater still poised between the knitting needles in Susy Hendrix's apartment.

136: Audrey Hepburn Estate Collection, 1953

Most likely a hair and makeup test for *Sabrina*, Audrey stands statuesque under the studio lighting, exhibiting her trademark calm and delicate demeanor.

"God kissed her on the cheek," director Billy Wilder once said, "and there she was."

137: Bob Willoughby, 1953

Bob Willoughby shoots photographer Bud Fraker shooting Audrey with his large format 8x10 studio portrait camera. Willoughby describes his first glimpse of Audrey as "this vision swathed in voile" and admits he started rifling through his equipment so as to regain "a modicum of composure."

Although, as a second-stringer, Willoughby might have casually watched Fraker set up, he confesses that his eyes "kept drifting back to that face. It was a different face, for sure, but . . . I couldn't quite put my finger on what it was. It was definitely something special."

139: Douglas Kirkland, 1965

How divine! Audrey, with be-glittered eyelids closed, in her *How to Steal a Million* black lace cocktail dress. Douglas Kirkland shot a series of these Audrey close-ups in which, eyes opened or closed, Audrey has the relaxed manner of one who has been lulled into each perfect pose.

"Totally hip before it was hip to be hip," Sean says, "or maybe even before it actually existed!"

141: Audrey Hepburn Estate Collection, circa 1970

In this blown-out version of Audrey, her doe eyes take center stage. "Without a doubt, one of my favorite photos," Sean says. "Timeless—ethereal, powdery Japanese porcelain and China ink." Today, women around the world discuss how to achieve "Audrey eyes," still holding her in the highest esteem as a model of inner and outer beauty.

142–143: Mark Shaw, 1954

Mark Shaw elicits the most delightful expression from Audrey, who models for a 1954 *Mademoiselle* magazine article. "True joy—light heartfelt elation," says Sean of his mother. Shaw liked "a natural look and in order to keep his subject relaxed he worked with as little photo-graphic equipment as possible." In this Shaw photo, it seems that there's hardly anything but Audrey.

144: Philippe Halsman, 1955

Halsman manages to connect directly with Audrey, whose calm and gentle nature seen here is reflected in the background by a pair of doves.

Halsman believed his job as a photographer was part psychologist. "I do not direct the sitter—the only thing I try is to help him over his fears and inhibitions. I try to capture what I feel reflects something of his inner life," Halsman said.

This particular Halsman was chosen for the cover of Sean's best-selling 2003 book, *An Elegant Spirit: A Son Remembers*.

145: Philippe Halsman, 1955

One of a series of photos Halsman took of Audrey at La Vigna, utilizing both the farm setting and its inhabitants. Both Audrey and the dove sit quietly, seemingly contemplating the presence of each other.

146: Mark Shaw, 1953

Shaw finds Audrey studying her *Sabrina* script in her studio bungalow on the Paramount lot.

"If I'm honest I have to tell you that I still read fairy tales," Audrey said, "and I like them best of all." That might explain why Audrey was so attracted to transformational characters, like those in *Roman Holiday*, *Sabrina*, *Funny Face*, and *My Fair Lady*.

147: Mark Shaw, 1953

"The tiniest waist . . . ever!" remarks Sean about his mother in this Shaw photo. It measured 20 inches to be exact, and Givenchy said that over nearly forty years, he never had to adjust the original proportions on the mannequin used to fit her designs.

In an oft-quoted poem attributed to Audrey, but written by American writer, humorist, and teacher Sam Levenson, we are reminded, "For a slim figure, share your food with the hungry."

149: John Engstead, 1953

In 1953, Audrey appeared wearing a kerchief in *Roman Holiday* and unwittingly sparked a fashion trend embraced by headscarf-wearing fans around the world. Stores could hardly keep them in stock and began offering them by mail order so as to keep up with the demand. "Just a scarf and it's forever," remarks Sean.

Later, when Audrey tails co-star Cary Grant in *Charade*, she pairs her headscarf with oversized sunglasses, harking back to that first "Audrey Look," introduced in *Breakfast at Tiffany's*.

151: Bob Willoughby, 1958

"A different hat, a different expression, and—voilá—from Rima the forest nymph to a Western belle," remarked photographer Bob Willoughby.

Looking at this photo, Luca remembers, "I used to ask her to play a mean character in a movie for once, like an evil lady in a James Bond 007 movie. She replied that she didn't 'fit the part,' but I still think she does."

152–153: Mel Ferrer, 1954

"She loved the silence of the mountains blanketed in snow," Luca says of his mother. It gave her "the peace she always sought."

"After years of hard work and the depletions caused by the war, she was anemic and exhausted," says Sean. "My father came up with the idea of the 'mountains.' So, they rented the house in Bürgenstock, perched right above Lake Lucerne. The fresh air and altitude would help bring her back to health."

Eventually the Ferrers settled down in an eighteenth-century farmhouse called "La Paisible," which translates to "the peaceful place." Situated on three acres near Lake Geneva in Switzerland, it was surrounded by mature orchards and flowering gardens.

155: Douglas Kirkland, circa 1975

Luca calls this photo of Audrey, "La Mamma of my youth." Taken in the mid-1970s, Audrey's hair and sunglasses reflect the latest styles of the time, trends she helped perpetuate.

"Audrey's every expression could speak volumes," Rob Wolders adds. "Here," Rob says, "Douglas Kirkland captures her subtle radiance and spontaneous zest." The photographic equipment, a chair, and a couple of onlookers can be seen mirrored in the lenses of Audrey's fabulous oversized sunglasses.

157: Sanford Roth, circa 1958

Sanford Roth photographs Audrey in St. Moritz standing in front of the sleigh taken for a ride through the Swiss winter wonderland. Roth was an accomplished photographer with an impressive roster of the most important celebrities in Europe and Hollywood. He shot for every major European and American magazine and his photographs were collected by, among many others, two of Audrey's dear friends, Jean Cocteau and *Gigi* author Colette.

158–159: Betty Press, 1992

Taken in 1992 in Kenya, Audrey is surrounded by children who know nothing of her fame but everything about her kindness. "After her trips," Luca says, "she would only talk about the joy, the smiles these people had. She couldn't accept the loss of even one of these smiles."

As a UNICEF International Goodwill Ambassador, Audrey worked continuously until the end of her life to "speak for those children who cannot speak for themselves." Sean calls this photo "her legacy."

161: Robert Wolders, 1989

Rob Wolders accompanied Audrey as she traveled sometimes rugged and dangerous terrain all over the world. In 1989, on a trip to the Sudan, he snapped this photo of Audrey. Later, Audrey would reflect about her work, saying, "During the past years I have traveled the world and seen these children, so many of them, leading lives of tremendous pain. And yet, they retain their sweetness and their patience; their eyes reflect a deeper understanding, an awareness that this is not as it should be."

This photo, among her favorites, was kept framed at her home in Switzerland.

163: John Isaac, 1988

UNICEF photographer John Isaac accompanied Audrey on many of her trips over the years. This photo was taken in early 1988 during Audrey's first field mission to Ethiopia.

Rob remembers, "We had traveled from Addis Ababa to the northern region of the country, which had been much affected by drought and famine. Early one morning we visited a refugee camp comprised mostly of young children, their parents having perished in the famine or as victims of the civil war. As always, the children flocked around Audrey and as she knelt down to speak to one child, another embraced her from the back. As she rose, the child continued to cling to her, resulting in this glorious image."

John Isaac remains a treasured family friend.

165: Robert Wolders, 1991

"This photo was taken in the spring of 1991 when the *Koolzaad*-fields (mustard fields) adjacent to the house in Switzerland were in full bloom," says Rob. "We habitually used to take our daily walks on the paths along the fields and the two small Jack Russells loved to run through the tall stalks, often refusing to come out, making us chase them. On this occasion, Audrey had just retrieved both dogs at the same time. She called her dog, Penny, "the poet" because of her gentle nature, and Missy, my dog, "the ragamuffin," because of her mischievousness. This photo tugs at my heartstrings the most because it shows Audrey in the surroundings she most loved, where she was truly at home."

Sean points out that in this photo his mother wears her UNICEF sweatshirt.

The Audrey Hepburn Children's Fund

In 1988, Audrey Hepburn embarked on what she considered her most important career, as a UNICEF International Goodwill Ambassador. She dedicated her last five years to this unending humanitarian work, traveling throughout the developing world in order to present a firsthand and provocative vision of children in pain, struggling to survive, or just fighting for basic human rights.

In 1994, the Audrey Hepburn Children's Fund was created by her sons, Sean and Luca, and long-time love, Robert Wolders, in order to commemorate and continue her humanitarian legacy.

Today, the Audrey Hepburn Children's Fund supports many organizations in the United States and around the world dedicated to helping improve the lives of children through a variety of programs, projects, and initiatives.

Please visit **www.audreyhepburn.com** to learn more about what the Fund does and how you can participate.

Author Bios

Ellen (Erwin) Fontana grew up in Winthrop, Massachusetts, a small seacoast town near Boston. She received her Bachelor of Arts and Master of Fine Arts degrees in Dramatic Arts from the University of California, Davis.

A veteran of over twenty-five years in the film industry, she began her career at a major Los Angeles talent agency where she worked in the literary departments for television and feature films. She went on to work at Paramount Pictures, Twentieth Century Fox, and Universal Studios, where she learned the art of moviemaking and the craft of writing for film. Ellen has produced for film, television, and is also a screenwriter. Recently Ellen co-wrote the six-part mini-series *Cloudstreet*, based on Tim Winton's best-selling Australian novel, currently filming in western Australia. She was also a contributing author on the book version of the independent cult hit movie *What the Bleep Do We Know!?* and edited a children's book on quantum physics entitled *Dr. Quantum and the Grandfather Paradox*. Ellen co-authored *The Audrey Hepburn Treasures*, a scrapbook biography on the life and career of actress, icon, and humanitarian Audrey Hepburn.

Ellen lives in Los Angeles with her husband, Enzo Fontana, an Italian fine art painter, and has one daughter, Zoe-Ruth Erwin. Ellen has worked at the Audrey Hepburn Children's Fund since 2000 and has been the Executive Director since 2002.

Sean Hepburn Ferrer was born in Lucerne, Switzerland, on July 17, 1960, to to Audrey and Mel Ferrer.

In 1963, the family moved to the Lake Geneva area. Sean continued to travel with his parents, living in Italy, Spain, England, France, and the United States until he started school in 1965. His parents separated and subsequently divorced in the late sixties, and by 1970 Sean had moved to Rome to live with his mother and her second husband, Andrea Dotti, an Italian psychiatrist. Sean attended the Lycée Chateaubriand and in the mid-seventies he was enrolled in Le Rosey, a private Swiss boarding school, where he completed his education with a French Baccalaureate.

After only a semester at the University of Geneva's international law school, Sean was offered a job on a major motion picture by Terence Young, the legendary creator of James Bond for the big screen.

What was going to be a sabbatical became a career. For thirty-two years, Sean has worked in every aspect of the entertainment arena, from film and television development and production and marketing to the management of IPs and their related commercial applications. With his partner Paul Alberghetti, Sean owns and operates Licensing Artists LLC, an agency dedicated to the management of legacy-related intellectual properties. He is the chairman and founder of the Audrey Hepburn Children's Fund, a 501(c)(3) public non-profit. Both businesses are headquartered in Pasadena, California.

Sean lives in Florence, Italy, with his wife and three children.

Luca Dotti was born in Lausanne, Switzerland, on February 8, 1970, to Audrey and Andrea Dotti. He attended the French Lycée in Rome, receiving his Baccalaureate in 1988.

Luca studied graphic design and typography in Italy and France and worked for design studios in Milan and Paris. He has been a freelance designer since 1999.

Luca lives in Rome, Italy, with his wife and two children.

"A farmer grows, a gardener prunes." —Luca Dotti

Robert Wolders was born in Rotterdam, Holland, on September 28, 1936. Rob lived in Holland through the occupation during World War II—only about twenty miles from where Audrey spent the war.

In the mid 1950s, Rob moved to the United States, attending the University of Rochester, New York University, and the American Academy of Dramatic Arts. After completing his education, Rob worked at Universal Studios for a number of years before becoming involved in real estate investing. He was formally introduced to Audrey at the home of their mutual friend Connie Wald in 1980, and he and Audrey remained together for the rest of her life.

Acknowledgments

This book would not be possible without the personal, thoughtful, and generous contributions made by the Audrey Hepburn Estate, in particular Rob Wolders, Sean Hepburn Ferrer, and Luca Dotti, who spent countless hours reviewing and discussing the photos chosen to include in this book.

Sincere thanks and appreciation to the Audrey Hepburn Children's Fund, to Paul Alberghetti and Caroline S. Bloxsom, and to Nicole Slovinsky for her dedication and research.

Special thanks to our team at becker&mayer!, specifically, our editor, Kristin Mehus-Roe; photo researcher, Shayna Ian; and designer, Joanna Price. Their patience and support made this a truly unique experience and resulted in a book we are all excited about and pleased to present.

—Ellen Fontana

Sources

Books and Periodicals

Beaton, Cecil. *Self-Portrait with Friends—The Selected Diaries of Cecil Beaton 1922–1974*. Times Books, 1979.

Conant, Howell. *Audrey Hepburn in* Breakfast at Tiffany's *and Other Photographs*. Schirmer/Mosel Munich, 2007.

Cripps, Charlotte. "Observations: Proud family reveals iconic encounters with the stars," *The Independent*. (April 24, 2009).

Erwin, Ellen and Jessica Z. Diamond. *The Audrey Hepburn Treasures*. Atria Books, 2006.

Karney, Robyn. *A Star Danced—The Life of Audrey Hepburn*. Bloomsbury Publishing Ltd., 1993.

Levenson, Sam. *In One Era & Out the Other*. Simon & Schuster, 1973.

Long, Carola. "Shooting star: The extraordinary unseen photographs of Paul Newman," *The Independent*. (August 29, 2009).

Paris, Barry. *Audrey Hepburn*. Berkley Books, 1996.

Rayfield, Stanley. *How* Life *Gets the Story: Behind the scenes in photo-journalism*. Doubleday & Company, 1955.

Shaw, Mark. *Charmed by Audrey—Life on the Set of Sabrina*. CITY: Insight Editions, 2008

Sulcas, Roslyn. "The Week Ahead," *New York Times* (November 8, 2009).

Remembering Audrey 15 Years Later—Photographs by Bob Willoughby (Life Great Photographers Series). Time Inc. Home Entertainment (Vol. 8, Number 1).

Web Sites

Archer, Eugene. "With a Little Bit of Luck and Plenty of Talent," http://audreyhepburnlibrary.com/mfl/images/mflscrapbkkpg25.jpg

"Audrey Hepburn—The Quintessential Style Icon." www.fashion.ie (3/26/10)

Emil Schulthess: Photographer 1913–1996. www.emil-schulthess.ch (3/19/10)

Female Celebrity Smoking List—Hepburn. http://smokingsides.com/asfs/H/Hepburn.html (3/23/10)

Mary Panzer, Curator of Photographs, National Portrait Gallery, Smithsonian Institution.

The Movie Projector—R. d. Finch Writes about Movies. http://movieprojector.blogspot.com/2009/10/i-love-paris-billy-wllders-love-in.html (3/24/10)

Philippe Halsman: A Retrospective. www.npg.si.edu/exh/Halsman/intro.htm

Philippe Halsman. http://en.wikipedia.org/wiki/Philippe_Halsman (3/20/10)

Sanford H. Roth. http://en.wikipedia.org/wiki/Sanford_H._Roth (3/26/10)

Yousuf Karsh. www.karsh.org (3/19/10)

www.audrey1.org/biography/17/audrey-hepburn-timeline-1950-1959 (3/20/10)

Image Credits

Every effort has been made to trace copyright holders. If any unintended omissions have been made, becker&mayer! would be pleased to add appropriate acknowledgment in future editions.

Front cover: Photo courtesy of mptvimages.com

Back cover: Photo by Antony Beauchamp / Audrey Hepburn Estate Collection
© Sean Ferrer and Luca Dotti

Pages 10–11: Audrey Hepburn Estate Collection © Sean Ferrer & Luca Dotti

Page 12: Courtesy of the Cecil Beaton Studio Archive at Sotheby's

Page 13: Courtesy of the Cecil Beaton Studio Archive at Sotheby's

Page 14: Courtesy of the Cecil Beaton Studio Archive at Sotheby's

Page 15: Courtesy of the Cecil Beaton Studio Archive at Sotheby's

Page 17: Courtesy of the Cecil Beaton Studio Archive at Sotheby's

Page 18: Courtesy of the Cecil Beaton Studio Archive at Sotheby's

Page 19: Courtesy of the Cecil Beaton Studio Archive at Sotheby's

Page 20: Photo by Hans Gerber, courtesy of ETH-Bibliothek Zurich,
Image Archive

Page 21: Photo by Hans Gerber, courtesy of ETH-Bibliothek Zurich,
Image Archive

Page 23: Photo by Pierluigi Praturlon © Reporters Associati - Roma

Page 24: © Philippe Halsman / Magnum Photos

Page 25: © Emil Schulthess / Swiss Foundation for Photography

Page 27: © Condé Nast Archive / Corbis

Pages 28–29: Audrey Hepburn Estate Collection © Sean Ferrer & Luca Dotti

Page 31: Photo by Sam Shaw © 1996 Sam Shaw, Inc., licensed by
Shaw Family Archives, Ltd.

Page 32: Norman Parkinson Archive

Page 33: Norman Parkinson Archive

Page 34: Photo by Mel Ferrer, Audrey Hepburn Estate Collection
© Sean Ferrer & Luca Dotti

Page 35: Photo by Mel Ferrer, Audrey Hepburn Estate Collection
© Sean Ferrer & Luca Dotti

Page 37: © 1978 Leo Fuchs / mptvimages.com

Pages 38–39: © 1978 Leo Fuchs / mptvimages.com

Page 41: © 1978 Leo Fuchs / mptvimages.com

Page 43: Courtesy of the Cecil Beaton Studio Archive at Sotheby's

Page 44: Audrey Hepburn Estate Collection © Sean Ferrer & Luca Dotti

Page 45: © Willy Rizzo

Page 47: © David Seymour / Magnum Photos

Pages 48–49: Courtesy of the Cecil Beaton Studio Archive at Sotheby's

Page 50: Courtesy of the Cecil Beaton Studio Archive at Sotheby's

Page 51: Cecil Beaton/Condé Nast Archive; Copyright © Condé Nast

Page 53: © Yousuf Karsh

Pages 54–55: Audrey Hepburn Estate Collection © Sean Ferrer & Luca Dotti

Page 57: © 2000 Mark Shaw / mptvimages.com

Page 58: © 2000 Mark Shaw / mptvimages.com

Page 59: © 2000 Mark Shaw / mptvimages.com

Page 60: Photos by Mel Ferrer, Audrey Hepburn Estate Collection
© Sean Ferrer & Luca Dotti

Page 61: Photo by Mel Ferrer, Audrey Hepburn Estate Collection
© Sean Ferrer & Luca Dotti

Page 62: Photo by Sam Shaw © 2010 Sam Shaw, Inc., licensed by
Shaw Family Archives, Ltd.

Page 63: Photo by Sam Shaw © 2010 Sam Shaw, Inc., licensed by
Shaw Family Archives, Ltd.

Page 65: Audrey Hepburn Estate Collection © Sean Ferrer & Luca Dotti

Pages 66–67: © Douglas Kirkland / Corbis

Page 69: © Douglas Kirkland / Corbis

Pages 70–71: © Paramount Pictures. All Rights Reserved

Page 73: mptvimages.com

Pages 74–75: Inge Morath © The Inge Morath Foundation / Magnum Photos

Page 76: © Sunset Boulevard / Corbis

Page 77: © Sunset Boulevard / Corbis

Page 79: Audrey Hepburn Estate Collection © Sean Ferrer & Luca Dotti

Page 80: © Philippe Halsman / Magnum Photos

Page 81: © Philippe Halsman / Magnum Photos

Page 83: © Philippe Halsman / Magnum Photos

Pages 84–85: Photo by Pierluigi Praturlon © Reporters Associati - Roma

Page 87: © 2000 Mark Shaw / mptvimages.com

Page 89: © Norman Parkinson / Sygma / Corbis

Page 91: Audrey Hepburn Estate Collection © Sean Ferrer & Luca Dotti

Page 93: Photo by Pierluigi Praturlon © Reporters Associati - Roma

Page 95: © 1978 Leo Fuchs / mptvimages.com

Pages 96–97: Audrey Hepburn Estate Collection © Sean Ferrer & Luca Dotti

A NOTE ON THE TYPE

Audrey 100 is composed largely in the san serif typeface Gotham. First used to convey masculinity by *GQ* magazine, Gotham was designed by Tobias Frere-Jones and Jesse Ragan. The typeface takes inspiration from the traditional signage seen on mid-century buildings in New York City. The typeface is widely used, most recently and conspicuously in the political advertising for Barack Obama's presidential campaign.

Titles are in the neoclassical font known as Didot, named after the reputed French printing and type-producing family who developed the original collection of Didot types in the period 1784-1811. The typeface takes inspiration from John Baskerville's experimentation with increased stroke contrast and condensed armature, evoking the Age of Enlightenment.

Printed and bound in China through Imago.

Interior designed by Joanna Price.